ISBN: 9781313545730

Published by:
HardPress Publishing
8345 NW 66TH ST #2561
MIAMI FL 33166-2626

Email: info@hardpress.net
Web: http://www.hardpress.net

d Brief Reply, p. 11.

Priv. Coun., Ser. iii er. 44L. Ban

unt., iii

s of Parliament (Thomson), ix. 269.

Coun., iii. vii. 31.

mond's Annals of Sc.

er, lv

*onn., iii. vii. 31.
nond's *Annals of Sc.*
er, lv

between Mr. Anderson and the other printers did not

to a ... ... ring ... twenty

etween M⸺ derson and ⸺ other printers did no
to a⸺ ring t⸺ venty⸺

Anderson wa
Magist
D

ImTheStory.com

Personalized Classic Books in many genre's

Unique gift for kids, partners, friends, colleagues

Customize:

- Character Names
- Upload your own front/back cover images (optional)
- Inscribe a personal message/dedication on the
  inside page (optional)

Customize many titles Including
- Alice in Wonderland
- Romeo and Juliet
- The Wizard of Oz
- A Christmas Carol
- Dracula
- Dr. Jekyll & Mr. Hyde
- And more...

Lightning Source UK Ltd.
Milton Keynes UK
UKHW020951130720
366454UK00017B/1661